DETROIT RED WINGS

By Craig Zeichner

The Child's World®

THE CHILD'S WORLD®
1980 Lookout Drive • Mankato, MN 56003-1705
800-599-READ • www.childsworld.com

ACKNOWLEDGMENTS

The Child's World®: Mary Berendes, Publishing Director
Shoreline Publishing Group, LLC: James Buckley, Jr.,
  Production Director
The Design Lab: Gregory Lindholm, Design and
  Page Production

PHOTOS

Cover: AP/Wide World
Interior: AP/Wide World: 5, 6, 10, 17, 25 (3), 26, 27;
  Getty Images: 9, 18, 21, 22

LIBRARY OF CONGRESS
CATALOGING-IN-PUBLICATION DATA

Zeichner, Craig.
  Detroit Red Wings / by Craig Zeichner.
      p. cm.
  Includes bibliographical references and index.
  ISBN 978-1-60253-439-1 (library bound : alk. paper)
  1. Detroit Red Wings (Hockey team)—History—Juvenile
literature. I. Title.

  GV848.D47Z45 2010
  796.962'640977434—dc22

2010015294

Printed in the United States of America
Mankato, Minnesota
July 2010
F11538

TABLE OF CONTENTS

GO, RED WINGS!

A player in a Red Wings **sweater** zips down the ice. He quickly stops in front of the net. When he stops, his skates scrape the ice, sending ice chips flying in the air. He blasts the **puck** into the net for a Red Wings goal. The Red Wings win! Red Wings players raise their sticks and celebrate! Let's meet the Detroit Red Wings.

The Detroit Red Wings celebrate another big goal.

Hockey players always battle. Kris Draper of the Red Wings shoves the Toronto Maple Leafs' Anton Stralman to the ice in a fight for the puck.

WHO ARE THE DETROIT RED WINGS?

The Detroit Red Wings play in the National Hockey League (NHL). They are one of 30 teams in the NHL. The NHL includes the Eastern Conference and the Western Conference. The Red Wings play in the Central Division of the Western Conference. The playoffs end with the winners of the Eastern and Western conferences facing off. The champion wins the **Stanley Cup**. The Red Wings have won 11 Stanley Cups.

WHERE THEY CAME FROM

The Red Wings first skated in the NHL in 1926. When they joined the league, their name was the Cougars. They became the Red Wings in 1932, and changed their **logo**. It shows a car tire with a wing, because many cars are made in Detroit. The Red Wings were one of the Original Six—the earliest members of the NHL. The team won their first Stanley Cup in 1936. They have won the most Stanley Cups of any NHL team from the United States.

Outdoor hockey? In 2009, the Red Wings faced the Blackhawks in a special game played at Chicago's Wrigley Field.

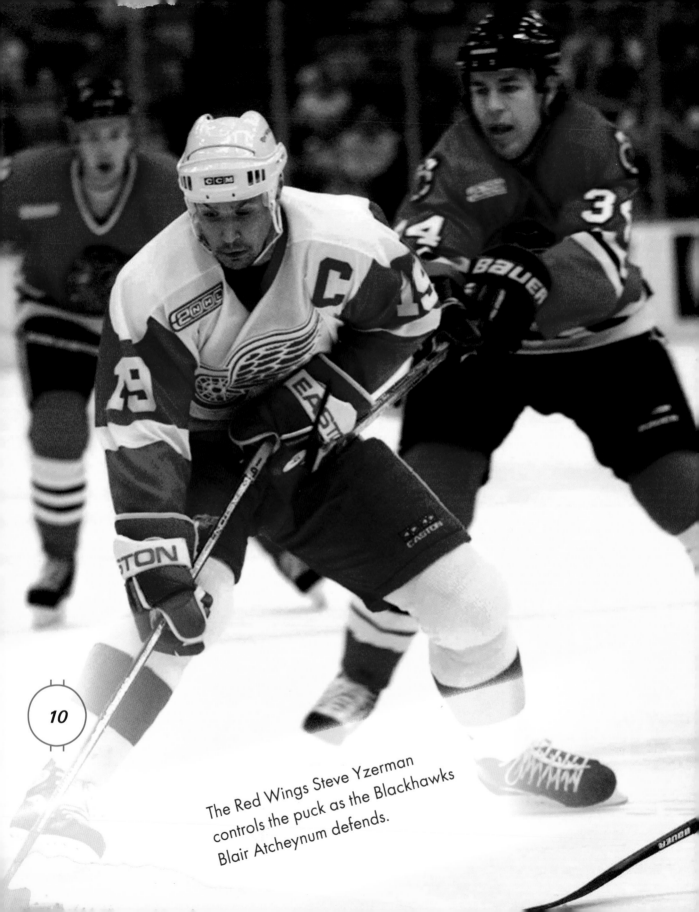

The Red Wings Steve Yzerman controls the puck as the Blackhawks Blair Atcheynum defends.

WHO THEY PLAY

The Detroit Red Wings play 82 games each season. They play all the other teams in their division six times. The other Central Division teams are the Chicago Blackhawks, the Columbus Blue Jackets, the Nashville Predators, and the St. Louis Blues. The Red Wings and the Blackhawks are fierce **rivals**. The Red Wings also play other teams in the Western and Eastern Conferences.

WHERE THEY PLAY

The Red Wings play their home games in Detroit's Joe Louis **Arena**. The arena is named after Joe Louis, one of the greatest boxers in history. The arena is also used for college hockey, boxing, wrestling, and concerts. The Joe Louis Arena's nickname is "the Joe." The Red Wings won two of their Stanley Cups at the Joe, in 1997 and 2002. Gordie Howe played in the 1980 NHL All-Star game there when he was 51 years old. The fans cheered loudly for him. There is a large statue of Howe in the hallway of the arena.

A bronze statue of Gordie Howe greets you when you come to the Joe Louis Arena. Howe was one of the greatest players in NHL history.

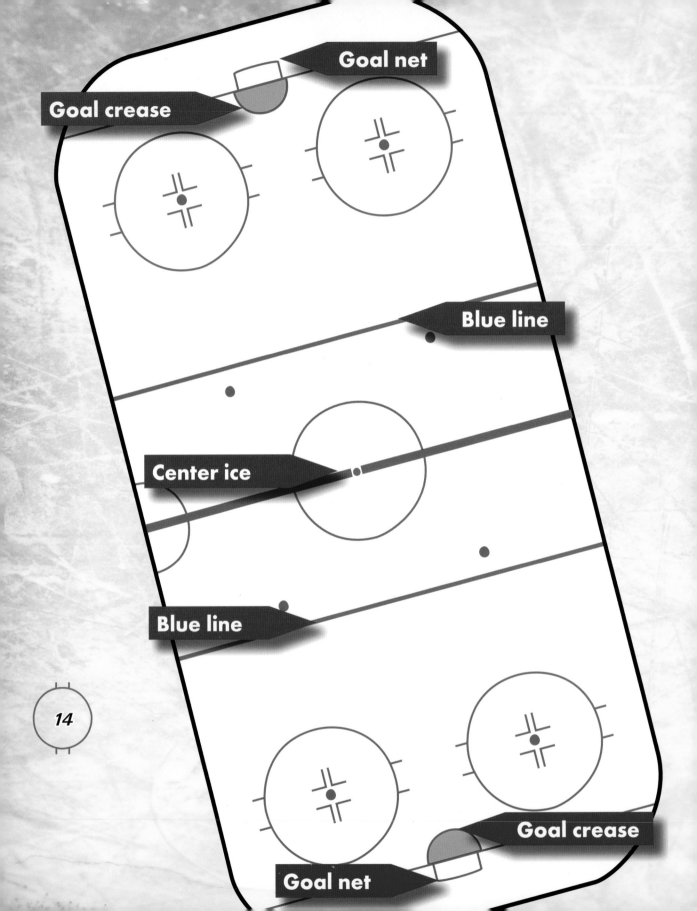

Goal net

Goal crease

Blue line

Center ice

Blue line

Goal crease

Goal net

14

THE HOCKEY RINK

Hockey games are played on a sheet of ice called a rink. It is a rounded rectangle. NHL rinks are 200 feet (61 m) long and 85 feet (26 m) wide. Wooden boards surround the entire rink. Clear plastic panels are on top of the boards so fans can see the action and be protected from flying pucks. Netting is hung above the seats at each end of the rink to catch any wild pucks. The goal nets are near each end of the rink. Each net is four feet (1.2 m) high and six feet (1.8 m) wide. A red line marks the center of the ice. Blue lines mark each team's defensive zone.

THE PUCK

An NHL puck is made of very hard rubber. The disk is three inches (76 mm) wide and 1 inch (25 mm) thick. It weighs about 6 ounces (170 g). It's black so it's easy to see on the ice. Many pucks are used during a game, because some fly into the stands.

15

BIG DAYS!

The Red Wings have had many great seasons in their long history. Here are three of the greatest.

1935–36: Led by **wing** John Sorrell, the Red Wings won their first Stanley Cup championship.

1951–52: Gordie Howe had one of his greatest seasons. He scored 47 goals and 39 **assists**. Howe and the great **goalie** Terry Sawchuk were the stars as the Red Wings won their fifth Stanley Cup.

1996–97: The Red Wings won their eighth Stanley Cup. It was their first championship in 42 years!

Center Sergei Fedorov lifts the Stanley Cup in 1997. Fedorov was the Red Wings' top scorer in the 1997 playoffs.

The Red Wings Darren McCarty is knocked to the ice by the Kings' Jere Karalahti. The Kings beat the Red Wings in the 2001 playoffs.

TOUGH DAYS!

Not every season can end with a Stanley Cup championship. Here are some of the toughest seasons in Red Wings history.

1967–68: The Red Wings played 70 games but only won 22! They did not make it to the playoffs.

1970–71: The Red Wings finished in last place in their division. They gave up 308 goals during the season.

2000–01: The Red Wings had a great season and finished with 111 **points**. But they lost to the Los Angeles Kings in the first round of the playoffs.

MEET THE FANS

Detroit Red Wings fans are crazy about their team! The fans love their team so much, they call Detroit "Hockeytown." The Red Wings fans have one of the NHL's most famous traditions. During important games, a fan will toss an octopus onto the ice. Yuck! This first happened during the 1952 playoffs. In those days, it took eight games to win the Stanley Cup and an octopus has eight arms. The fans think it's good luck. It must be, since the Red Wings have won so many Stanley Cups.

A Red Wings fan wears an octopus doll on his head. It's not as gross as carrying a real octopus around!

21

Gordie Howe is the Red Wings' greatest scorer and the third highest scorer in NHL history.

HEROES THEN...

Many players in the **Hockey Hall of Fame** skated for the Red Wings. Wing Gordie Howe was the leading scorer in the NHL for many years. He was tough and had a great shot. Howe played for a long time and once played on the same team with two of his sons. Howe's nickname is "Mr. Hockey." Terry Sawchuk was one of the greatest goalies in the NHL. In the 1952 Stanley Cup playoffs, he did not give up any goals in four games! **Captain** Steve Yzerman and wing Brendan Shanahan led the Red Wings to win the Stanley Cup in 1997. It was the first Red Wings Stanley Cup in 42 years.

HEROES NOW...

The Red Wings have some of the top players in the NHL. Nicklas Lidstrom has won the James Norris trophy six times. The trophy is for the NHL's best **defensemen**. Lidstrom is now the Red Wings captain. Henrik Zetterberg is one of the NHL's most skilled players. Zetterberg is an excellent skater and a top scorer. Defenseman Brian Rafalski is one of the best players from the United States. Rafalski is known for his very hard shot. Center Pavel Datsyuk is a fine defensive player and is great at passing the puck. Wing Kris Draper is a veteran player who knocks his opponents to the ice with hard hits.

WING

HENRIK ZETTERBERG

DEFENSEMAN

NICKLAS LIDSTROM

WING

PAVEL DATSYUK

25

GEARING UP

Hockey players wear short pants and a jersey called a "sweater." Underneath, they wear lots of pads to protect themselves. They also wear padded gloves and a hard plastic helmet. They wear special ice hockey skates with razor-sharp blades. They carry a stick to handle the puck.

Goalies wear special gloves to help them block and catch shots. They have extra padding on their legs, chest, and arms. They also wear special decorated helmets and use a larger stick.

26

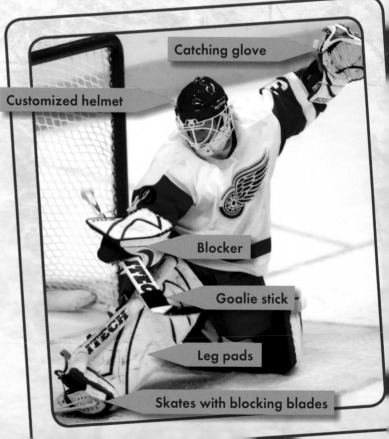

Catching glove

Customized helmet

Blocker

Goalie stick

Leg pads

Skates with blocking blades

Helmet

Face shield

Shoulder pads

Sweater

Gloves

Shin guards

Stick

Skates

SPORTS STATS

Here are some all-time career records for the Detroit Red Wings. All the stats are through the 2009–2010 season.

GOALS

HOT SHOTS

These players have scored the most career goals for the Red Wings.

PLAYER	GOALS
Gordie Howe	786
Steve Yzerman	692

ASSISTS

PERFECT PASSERS

These players have the most career assists on the team.

PLAYER	ASSISTS
Steve Yzerman	1,063
Gordie Howe	1,023

POINTS

BIG SCORES!

These players have the most points, a combination of goals and assists.

PLAYER	POINTS
Gordie Howe	1,809
Steve Yzerman	1,755

GOALS AGAINST AVERAGE

SUPER SAVERS

These Detroit goalies have allowed the fewest goals per game in their career.

PLAYER	GAA
Terry Sawchuk	2.44
Chris Osgood*	2.48

CAREER PLUS-MINUS

PLAYER POSITIVE

These players have the best **plus-minus** in Red Wings history.

PLAYER	PLUS-MINUS
Nicklas Lidstrom *	+431
Sergei Fedorov	+276

COACHES

FROM THE BENCH

These coaches have the most wins in Red Wings history.

COACH	WINS
Jack Adams	413
Scotty Bowman	410

29

GLOSSARY

arena an indoor place for sports

assists plays that give the puck to the player who scores a goal

captain a player chosen to lead his team on and off the ice

center a hockey position at the middle of the forward, offensive line

defensemen players who take a position closest to their own goal, to keep the puck out

goalie the goaltender, whose job is to keep pucks out of the net

Hockey Hall of Fame located in Toronto, Ontario, this museum honors the greatest players in the sport's history

logo a colorful design that stands for a sports team

plus-minus a player gets a plus one for being on the ice when their team scores a goal, and a minus one when the other team scores a goal; the total of these pluses and minuses creates this stat. The better players always have high plus ratings

points a team gets two points for every game they win and one point for every game they tie; a player gets a point for every goal he scores and another point for every assist

puck the hard, frozen rubber disk used when playing hockey

rivals teams that play each other often and with great intensity

Stanley Cup the trophy awarded each year to the winner of the National Hockey League championship

sweater a shirt or jersey worn by a hockey player

wing a hockey position on the outside left or right of the forward line

FIND OUT MORE

BOOKS

Goodman, Michael E. *Detroit Red Wings: NHL History & Heroes.*
Toronto: Saunders Book Co., 2009.

Leonetti, Michael. *A Hero Named Howe.* Vancouver: Raincoast
Books, 2006.

Thomas, Kelly, and John Kicksee. *Inside Hockey!: The Legends, Facts,
and Feats that Made the Game.* Toronto: Maple Leaf Press, 2008.

WEB SITES

Visit our Web page for links about the Detroit Red Wings and
other pro hockey teams.

childsworld.com/links

Note to Parents, Teachers, and Librarians: We routinely verify our
Web links to make sure they are safe, active sites—so encourage your
readers to check them out!

INDEX

ABOUT THE AUTHOR

Craig Zeichner has been going to hockey games since he was 11 years old. He roots for the New York Rangers but likes the Red Wings, too. Craig grew up playing roller hockey in Brooklyn, NY.